DAY OF TRAGEDY

September 11, 2001

The calm before the twin towers tragic disaster.
New York City, lower Manhattan, before 8:48 a.m, September 11, 2001

An unthinkable event happened to the United States of America and its citizens on September 11, 2001. Terrorists hijacked four passenger jet airliners, each carrying tanks full of fuel and large numbers of passengers, enroute to destinations in western United States. The hijackers commandeered the planes and deliberately flew three of the planes to points where destruction was achieved: the World Trade Center in New York City and the Pentagon in Arlington, Virginia, next to Washington, D.C., the nation's capital. The fourth plane crashed in a field near Shanksville, Pennsylvania, just north of Camp David, the Presidential Retreat in Maryland. Efforts by the hijackers to cause additional destruction was thwarted by the heroic passengers of the airliner. Thousands of people were killed; destruction of property soars in the billions of dollars; but the resolve of the American people has swelled to a massive crescendo of support for the country. America will achieve! America will persevere! America will stand steadfast and overcome the grievous loss it has sustained. To the families who have lost their loved ones; to the rescue workers who are undaunted and continue their efforts; to the volunteers who give endless hours of their time—America Salutes You!

As an historical publication, the pictures shown in the book illustrate the destruction, pain and suffering of the Day of Tragedy, September 11, 2001.

Published by American Products Publishing Company
6750 SW 111th Avenue
Beaverton, OR 97008

Text by: Barbara Shangle
Concept and Design by Robert D. Shangle
Printed in the United States of America
Copyright ©July, 2002, by Robert D. Shangle

Photography by Wide World Photos, Inc. and Associated Press, except this page and the upper left front cover image by James Blank
First Printing: July, 2002
ISBN 1-58583-144-1

The north tower of New York City's World Trade Center

A hijacked American Airlines passenger jet airliner crashed into the building on September 11, 2001, striking at 8:48 a.m. near the 95th floor. (AP Photo/Richard Drew)

A view of New York City's World Trade Center's north tower

Television viewers gazed in horror as this hijacked United Airlines passenger jet airliner thrust toward the south tower of the World Trade Center, located directly behind the north tower, striking the building at 9:03 a.m. (AP Photo/ABC via APTN) TV OUT: CBC OUT

The south tower of New York City's World Trade Center

The hijacked United Airlines jet airliner, Flight 175, was deliberately flown into the tower, striking the building at about the 90th floor. (AP Photo/Carmen Taylor)

The twin towers of the World Trade Center in New York City's lower Manhattan

The two 110-story steel and glass towers, designed by architects Minoru Yamasaki and Emery Roth, were vicously attacked on Tuesday morning, September 11, 2001. (AP Photo. Moshe Bursuker)

The twin towers of the World Trade Center complex

The three images above occurred in sequence a fraction of a second apart. In the top image, the airliner is a few feet from hitting the South Tower, the second tower to be hit by a jet airliner. In the middle image, the nose of the airliner has penetrated through the building to the opposite side of the south tower. The explosion caused by the collision is revealed in the third image. (AP Photo/ABC via APTN)

The World Trade Center

Two hijacked passenger airliners were deliberately flown into the twin towers of the World Trade Center by terrorists. The billowing black smoke from the north tower floats over the south tower that just sustained an impact by the highjacked United Airline jet airliner, Flight 175, having departed Logan International Airport in Boston, Massachusetts, destined for Los Angeles, California, carrying 65 people. (AP Photo/Chao Soi Cheong)

At the World Trade Center

It was 9:03 a.m. on September 11, 2001, when the jet airliner crashed into the south tower at the World Trade Center, adding to the horrific attack on the financial center of the world. (AP Photo/Carmen Taylor)

The skyline of lower Manhattan, New York City

Billowing black smoke is forced out of the twin towers where thousands of employees had prepared for a day of work on the morning of September 11, 2001. Two Boeing jet airliners crashed into the buildings with deadly force and full fuel tanks. (AP Photo/Jim Collins)

The north and south towers of the World Trade Center

Gaping holes release billowing smoke from the flaming inferno of the twin towers. (AP Photo)

The Empire State Building

From 1931 to 1973 the Empire State Building was the tallest building in New York City. In 1973 the twin towers of the World Trade Center complex rose elegantly upward, dwarfing the 102-story building that reached 1,250 feet in the air. On September 11, 2001, the smoking towers seen in the background soon crumbled, allowing the Empire State Building to regain the distinction of being the tallest building in the city. (AP Photo/Patrick Sison)

The south tower of the World Trade Center

At approximately 9:50 a.m. the south tower collapsed, bringing an end to a landmark in Manhattan and the end of life to several thousand people: employees and rescue workers, and guests. (AP Photo/Amy Sancetta)

The twin towers at the World Trade Center in lower Manhattan

The south tower begins to crumble into a mound of rubble, about forty-seven minutes after it was hit by a hijacked jet airliner flying at full force. The collapse of the building brought death and destruction beyond belief. (AP Photo/Jim Collins)

The twin towers of the World Trade Center

The collapse of the south tower occurred approximately forty-seven minutes after being struck by a powerful jet airliner traveling at some 500-miles per hour into the building, fully loaded with volatile jet fuel and carrying fifty-five people. (AP Photo/Jerry Torrens)

The south tower of the World Trade Center

The collapse of the tower sent debris and ash throughout Manhattan. Words cannot describe the horror and devastation experienced by onlookers as the building fell. An icon is no more. A death scene of war. A burial ground. (AP Photo/ Richard Drew)

A Plume of Disaster

Fear and terror encapsulate the expressions on the faces of those people running to escape the rushing cloud of dust and debris that rolled between the buildings toward open space. (AP Photo/Suzanne Plunkett)

The north tower: One World Trade Center, New York City, 10048

The smoldering north tower belches huge amounts of smoke while its companion tower crumbles to the ground, leaving only a memory. (AP Photo/David Karp)

New York City, September 11, 2001

Television viewers witnessed the awesome sight of the south tower of the World Trade Center collapse, sending rolls of billowing dust and debris throughout Manhattan. The destruction caused by terrorists flying two jet airliners into the twin towers staggered the citizens of the United States of America. (AP Photo/ABC)

Refugees of the Manhattan Attack, September 11, 2001

Gilded people hurry away from Ground Zero, the World Trade Center, in New York City. The horrifying attacks against the United States by a group of evil minded terrorists brought shock, humility, anger, fear, strength and severe sorrow to the resolute people of the nation. (AP Photo/Gulnara Samoilova)

Friends and Loved Ones Stick Together

A storm of debris caused by the collapse of the twin towers of the World Trade Center adds to the difficulty of escaping from the war-torn area of Manhattan. (AP Photo/Gulnara Samoilova)

Ruins of New York City's World Trade Center

Firefighters walk through the smoldering war zone.

The rubble of the World Trade Center

The rescue of fallen victims. (AP Photo/Beth A. Keiser)

The collapsed structure of the World Trade Center

Emergency personnel of New York City and the Port Authority of New York and New Jersey expand their search and rescue efforts within the building's rubble. (AP Photo/Lawrence Jackson)

Lower Manhattan

Billowing smoke rises from the remains of the World Trade Center three days after the September 11th attack by terrorists, leaving a zone now referred to by many as Ground Hero, honoring the heroic efforts by emergency workers and fallen victims. (AP Photo/pool, NYC Office of Emergency Management)

The smoldering World Trade Center, September 19, 2001

Ten days following the terrorist attack, smoke still rises from the collapsed World Trade Center in Manhattan. (AP Photo/Cameron Bloch)

"We Will Never Forget"

On September 24, 2001, the heavily damaged American Express building on West Street, facing the remains of one of the destroyed World Trade Center towers, is draped with a sign that expresses the thoughts of the nation's people: "We Will Never Forget." (AP Photo/Roberto Borea)

The burning debris of the World Trade Center, September 29, 2001

Hundreds of New York City police, Port Authority Police, New York City firemen and other support groups devoted endless hours searching for people in the debris caused by the collapse of the towers of the World Trade Center. Many of the victims of this war were members of the rescue parties. (AP Photo/Ed Betz)

The Cross at Ground Hero

This perfectly formed steel-beam cross was found by a laborer two days after the horrendous collapse of the twin towers of the World Trade Center. Now residing on the east side of the World Trade area as a permanent Symbol of Hope, this cross came from the rubble of One World Trade Center and maintains a revered position in the city. (AP Photo/Pool, Kathy Willens)

Twisted steel of the World Trade Center, Friday, February 1, 2002

The ravages of war blaze through the powdery dust and ash of the World Trade Center. Firemen and other rescue workers sift their way through tons of debris searching for victims of the reign of terror. (AP Photo/Virgil Case)

The Search and Rescue of Innocent Victims, March 2, 2002

Within the rubble of the World Trade Center, a priest prays over a body just removed from the rubble, surrounded by workers who pause from their work of searching for victims of the crash and collapse of the buildings. (AP Photo/ Louis Lanzano

The site of the World Trade Center disaster, New York City, March 8, 2002

A surviving city.

A Tablet of Loss as seen on April 9, 2002, at the World Trade Center

A registry of those heroes lost while struggling to save innocent victims stands in the rubble of the south tower. The Port Authority Police Department lost 37 people; there were 23 New York City police officers lost; the New York Fire Department firefighters lost 343 people. Comrades painted engine and ladder company numbers on the 58-ton steel beam. (AP Photo/Kathy Willens)

The site of the World Trade Center, New York City, as of May 1, 2002

The buildings of the World Financial Center loom over the vast emptiness of the World Trade Center.

Thursday, May 30, 2002, at the site of the World Trade Center

Homage smothers the air as the last steel beam from the World Trade Center site is removed during a ceremony that began precisely at 10:29 a.m., the exact time the south tower collapsed on September 11th. (AP Photo/Suzanne Plunkett)

At the tribute ceremony within the grounds of the World Trade Center

As an act of respect to victims unrecovered and still remaining within the site of the World Trade Center, an empty stretcher is carried by rescue personnel to a waiting ambulance during the "ceremony to officially end the recovery effort at the World Trade Center site in New York on Thursday, May 30, 2002." (AP Photo/David Rentas, pool)

At the Pentagon, September 11, 2001

"This photo from a Pentagon surveillance camera obtained on Thursday, March 7, 2002, shows the fireball that resulted when the hijacked American Airlines plane slammed into the Pentagon on Sept. 11. The image had been made available to law enforcement to aid in the investigation." (AP Photo)

The Pentagon, Arlington, Virginia, near Washington, D.C.

Terrorist flew a hijacked American Airlines jet airliner into the Pentagon about forty-five minutes after the second collision at the World Trade Center in New York City. (AP Photo/Tom Horan)

The Pentagon

Flames and smoke escape from the fiery furnace within the Pentagon, headquarters of the United States Department of Defense. The Pentagon states that approximately "23,000 military and civilian employees and about 3,000 non-defense support personnel" are housed within the facility. (AP Photo/Will Morris)

The Pentagon

The hijacked American Airlines jet airliner, Flight 77, carrying fifty-five people, flew directly into the west side of the Pentagon. Believed to have been originally destined for the White House, home to the nation's president, George W. Bush, the plane was somehow diverted. (AP Photo/The Daily Progress, Dan Lopez)

At the crash site of United Flight 93

"An aerial photo shows the crash site of United Flight 93 near Shanksville, Pa., taken by the FBI Wednesday, Sept. 19, 2001, and released Thursday, Sept. 20, 2001. The flight was hijacked by terrorists after taking off from Newark, N.J., Sept. 11, 2001. It crashed on the edge of a field killing all 44 aboard. Some of the passengers are believed to have fought their hijackers, keeping the plane from destroying a high-profile target in Washington...." (AP Photo/FBI)

A time of tribute to the passengers of United Flight 93

"A makeshift altar, constructed for a worship service, overlooks the crash site of United Airlines Flight 93, Sunday, Sept. 16, 2001, in Shanksville, PA. The plane was hijacked and crashed during [Sept. 11th] terrorist attacks. (AP Photo/Gene J. Puskar)

AFTERNOON EXTRA EDITION

THE CINCINNATI ENQUIRER

TUESDAY, SEPTEMBER 11, 2001

TERROR FROM THE AIR

U.S. ATTACKED

Hijacked airliners lead terrorist assault on World Trade Center, Pentagon

The Cincinnati Enquirer

To its readers in Cincinnati, Ohio, and beyond, the Cincinnati Enquirer printed the picture showing the explosion caused by the United Airlines jetliner, Flight 175, as it crashed into the south tower of the World Trade Center at 9:03 a.m. (AP Photo/Al Behrman)

The Los Angeles Daily News

Terror! That is what the Daily News reported in the extra edition provided for the West Coast readers regarding the devastating attack on the World Trade Center and the Pentagon, headquarters of the United States Department of Defense in Washington, D.C. (AP Photo/Reed Saxon)

Gallipolis Daily Tribune

Gallia County's Hometown Newspaper

50 CENTS • Vol. 108, No. 250 — TUESDAY, SEPTEMBER 11, 2001 — www.mydailytribune.com

TERROR IN THE HEARTLAND

THOUSANDS FEARED DEAD IN ATTACKS

Two planes slam World Trade Center

By Jerry Schwartz
AP NATIONAL WRITER

NEW YORK — Mounting an audacious attack against the United States, terrorists rashed two hijacked airliners into the World Trade Center and brought down the twin 110-story towers Tuesday morning. A jetliner also slammed into the Pentagon as the seat of government itself came under attack.

Hundreds were apparently killed aboard the jets, and untold numbers were feared dead in the rubble. Thousands were injured in New York.

A fourth jetliner, also apparently hijacked, crashed in Pennsylvania as the part of the closely timed series of attacks.

President Bush ordered a full-scale investigation to "hunt down the folks who committed this act."

Authorities were still trying to evacuate those who work in the twin towers when the glass-and-steel skyscrapers came down in a thunderous roar within about 90 minutes after the attacks, which took place 18 minutes apart around 9 a.m. Many people were feared trapped. About 50,000 people work at the Trade Center and tens of thousands of others visit each day.

Officials said the Trade Center apparently was pierced by two Los Angeles-bound jetliners that had been hijacked after taking off from Boston 15 minutes apart: first by American Flight 11, with 92 people aboard, then by United Flight 175, with 65 people on board.

The Pentagon was hit by American Flight 77, which was seized while carrying 64 people from Washington to Los Angeles, according to law enforcement officials, speaking on condition of anonymity.

And in Pennsylvania, United Flight 93, a Boeing 757 en route from Newark, N.J., to

Please see New York, 5

EXPLOSION — Smoke billows from one of the towers of the World Trade Center and flames and debris explode from the second tower today. In one of the most horrifying attacks ever against the United States, terrorists crashed two airliners into the World Trade Center in a deadly series of blows that brought down the twin 110-story towers. (AP Photo/Chao Soi Cheong)

Plane crashes into Pentagon

By Tom Raum
ASSOCIATED PRESS WRITER

WASHINGTON — The Pentagon took a direct, devastating hit from an aircraft, and enduring symbols of American power were evacuated Tuesday as an apparent terrorist attack spread fear and chaos in the nation's capital.

President Bush ordered the nation's military to "high-alert status" and prepared an evening televised address to a shaken nation. With the fires of destruction still burning administration officials said they suspected Osama bin Laden was the culprit behind parallel attacks in Washington and New York, where the World Trade Center collapsed into rubble with a heavy loss of life.

Bush vowed to "hunt down and punish those responsible."

The president, in Florida at the time of the attacks, flew home to the White House late in the day after stops at two

Please see Pentagon, 5

President Bush: 'We will pass this test'

Commander-in-chief responds to attack on freedom

By Sonya Ross
ASSOCIATED PRESS WRITER

BARKSDALE AIR FORCE BASE, La. — As chaos unhinged New York and Washington, President Bush was spirited from Florida to Louisiana to Nebraska — and then back to the nation's capital.

Bush planned to address the nation tonight.

"The resolve of our great nation is being tested. But make no mistake, we will show the world that we will pass this test," Bush declared earlier as terrorist strikes on the nation's centers of commerce and government forced him into virtual hiding.

He bounced between military installations here and in Nebraska, in what former

PRAYING — President Bush bows his head in a moment of silence during a brief appearance today at Emma E. Booker Elementary School in Sarasota, Fla. (AP Photo/St. Petersburg Times, Jennifer Davis)

President Clinton said was part of a Secret Service and military plan to keep the president safe.

"He needs to take every conceivable precaution in the event there are more attacks planned and there is a plan to attack the leadership of the United States," Clinton said in an interview.

The United States received no warning of the attacks on the Pentagon and New York, World Trade Center towers, White House press secretary Ari Fleischer said.

By teleconference, Bush joined a meeting of his National Security Council in Washington.

"Freedom itself was attacked

Please see Bush, 5

THE PENTAGON — Flames and smoke pour from a building Tuesday at the Pentagon after a direct, devastating hit from an aircraft. (AP Photo/Will Morris)

The Gallipolis Daily Tribune

Serving its readers since 1893, the Gallipolis Daily Tribune had this special edition of the newspaper out to its readers by 8 p.m. Tuesday, September 11, 2001. (AP/Gallipolis Daily Tribune)

The Advocate
A Gannett newspaper

Wednesday, September 12, 2001   A slice of life... **your life.**   Serving Licking County   35 cents

SPECIAL EDITION

TERRORISTS HIT HOME

American nightmare

Thousands dead in N.Y., D.C., Pa.; bin Laden suspected

NEW YORK (AP) — In the most devastating terrorist onslaught ever waged against the United States, knife-wielding hijackers crashed two airliners into the World Trade Center on Tuesday, toppling its twin 110-story towers. The deadly calamity was witnessed on televisions across the world as another plane slammed into the Pentagon, and a fourth crashed outside Pittsburgh.

"Today, our nation saw evil," President Bush said in an address to the nation Tuesday night. He said thousands of lives were "suddenly ended by evil, despicable acts of terror."

Said Adm. Robert J. Natter, commander of the U.S. Atlantic Fleet: "We have been attacked like we haven't since Pearl Harbor."

Establishing the death toll could take weeks. The four airliners alone had 266 people aboard and there were no known survivors. Arlington County, Va., fire chief said deaths at the Pentagon ranged between 100 and 800.

In addition, a union official said he feared 300 firefighters who first reached the scene had died in rescue efforts at the trade center — where 50,000 people worked — and dozens of police officers were missing.

"The number of casualties will be more than most of us can bear," a

14 pages of coverage inside

See Nightmare/10A

Locals worry about relatives

**By BRITTANY BAILEY,
KAREN VANCE
and KENT MALLETT
Advocate Reporters**

NEW YORK — About 9 a.m. Tuesday, Kelley Kremer was in an elevator on her way down from the fifth floor of one of the World Trade Center towers.

Suddenly, she felt the impact of a jetliner crashing into the building, and the elevator plunged several feet before safety brakes prevented a fall to ground level.

"So far she's OK," said her father, Robert Kremer, a Newark resident.

Still, news that she had survived the crash and the building's subsequent collapse turned somber when the second tower came crumbling down.

"I hope she was far enough away," Robert said early Tuesday afternoon.

Robert wasn't alone in his concern for friends and family. Many Licking County residents who watched the devastation were filled with fear and uncertainty.

While much of the country watched as a national tragedy unfolded, several area residents hoped minute-by-minute reports would tell them whether their loved ones were injured or killed.

It was the longest day Newark High School teachers June and Mike McCarthy have ever endured.

June McCarthy, a culinary arts teacher, and husband Mike, a social studies teacher, tried to

See Shock/10A

Smoke billows from one of the towers of the World Trade Center and flames and debris explode from the second tower, Tuesday. In one of the most horrifying attacks ever against the United States, terrorists crashed two airliners into the World Trade Center in a deadly series of blows that brought down the twin 110-story towers. *(AP Photo/Chao Soi Cheong)*

The second tower of the World Trade Center billows smoke after an airplane crashed into it.

The tower crumbles in a cascade of steel and concrete.

The collapse of the tower sends a huge cloud of smoke and dust through the city streets. *(Gannett News Service)*

Changes in today's Advocate

This edition is configured to allow for comprehensive coverage of Tuesday's attack on the United States. The entire A section is dedicated to coverage of the terrorist strikes. Local reaction and news can be found in section B. A condensed sports section appears in the back of section B, our Wednesday Food page on 1C, and Football Weekly in section D.

In addition, today's presstime was moved up several hours to allow for morning delivery. As of this time, our regular publicaton schedule will resume Thursday.

6   65503 00298
68550300298

Community Classifieds
3C and
www.ohiocommunityclass.com

Locals pray

With tears in many eyes, hundreds of local citizens attend prayer vigils and consoled each other Tuesday after watching America's worst day of terror on live television.

See page 1B

Talking to kids

How should you explain terrorist attacks to children? Also read about how local schools shared information with students on Tuesday.

See page 2B

Gas rush

Rumors of gas shortages and $5 per gallon prices prompted a run on local gas stations Tuesday night. Police were kept busy keeping order.

See page 2B

Sports halt

All local high school sports were canceled Tuesday and Ohio State University has postponed its Saturday football game until Oct. 20.

See page 8B

Series on hold

Publication of today's fourth installment of The Advocate's "God and Government" series" is being postponed to allow for expanded coverage of the attacks on America. It will appear at an undetermined later date.

The Advocate

In the early morning hours of September 12, 2001, the Special Edition of The Advocate newspaper of Newark, Ohio, provided a vivid description of the reign of terror on September 11, 2001. (AP Photo/The (Newark, Ohio) Advocate

45

AMERICA UNDER ATTACK: 20 PAGES OF COVERAGE

SPECIAL REPORT

THE INDIANAPOLIS STAR

Sunny
Low 57, high 83.
Page B12

"Where the Spirit of the Lord is, there is Liberty" II Cor. 3:17

State
Edition

A GANNETT NEWSPAPER   WEDNESDAY, SEPTEMBER 12, 2001   WWW.INDYSTAR.COM

DAY OF DEATH

■ **Legions feared dead:** An 'unbearable' number of lives lost; death toll impossible to calculate.

■ **Vengeance vowed:** Bush says 'freedom was attacked,' promises to hunt down those responsible.

■ **Buildings devastated:** Coordinated attacks level World Trade Center, ravage the Pentagon.

By Michael Grunwald
THE WASHINGTON POST

Terrorists unleashed an astonishing air assault on America's military and financial power centers Tuesday, hijacking four commercial jets and then crashing them into the World Trade Center in New York, the Pentagon in Washington and the Pennsylvania countryside.

It was by far the most devastating terrorist operation in U.S. history, killing thousands of people. It also was the most dramatic attack on U.S. soil since Pearl Harbor.

"Today, our nation saw evil," President Bush said in an address to the nation Tuesday night. He said thousands of lives were "suddenly ended by evil, despicable acts of terror."

Establishing the U.S. death toll could take weeks. The four airliners alone had 266 people aboard, and there were no known survivors. At the Pentagon, about 100 people were believed dead.

In addition, a firefighters union official said he feared an estimated 200 firefighters had died in rescue efforts at the Trade Center — where 50,000 people worked — and dozens of police officers were believed missing.

"The number of casualties will be more than most of us can bear," a visibly distraught Mayor Rudolph Giuliani said.

No one took responsibility for the attacks that rocked the seats of finance and government. But federal authorities identified Osama bin Laden, who has been given asylum by Afghanistan's Taliban rulers, as the prime suspect.

The attacks created indelible scenes of carnage and chaos, obliterating the World Trade Center's twin 110-story towers from their familiar perch above Manhattan's skyline, grounding the domestic air traffic system for the first time and plunging the entire nation into an unparalleled state of anxiety.

U.S. military forces at home and around the world were put on a "go to war" footing, the highest state of alert next to actual military action.

The Pentagon deployed a loose air defense network of warships along the West and East coasts, as well as an unspecified number of interceptor and reconnaissance aircraft to hunt for unauthorized planes and missiles.

The terrorists hijacked four California-bound flights from three airports on the Eastern seaboard, suggesting a well-financed, well-coordinated plot.

First, two jets slammed into the World Trade Center. Then an American Airlines flight out of Dulles International Airport ripped through the newly renovated

What's left of Trade Center: About 50,000 people worked at the World Trade Center, which collapsed shortly after its twin towers were struck by two jetliners. A firefighters union official said he feared 200 firefighters had died in rescue efforts at the Trade Center. Establishing the overall death toll could take weeks, authorities say. No one took responsibility for the attacks, but federal authorities have confirmed that they consider Osama bin Laden the prime suspect.

Corbis Sygma / Matthew McDermott

See DEATH Page 20

THE REACTION

Hoosiers cry, pray, buy guns
Watching the events left Hoosiers with a sense of disbelief. Many cried or prayed, and there was a rush on guns and TVs. **Page A5**

Americans anxious to help
Throughout the nation, landmarks closed, and people were overwhelmed with a desire to help the victims. **Page A5**

CENTRAL INDIANA

Could it happen here?
Indianapolis is vulnerable, but an attack is unlikely. Experts say terrorists might be tempted by the airport or Eli Lilly's headquarters but probably would favor higher-profile targets. **Page A13**

City comes to a startled halt
Indianapolis International Airport shut down. Downtown offices closed. Activity throughout Indianapolis was largely limited to lines at blood banks and gas stations. **Page A13**

Sports, concerts canceled
Baseball games were canceled, and football games are in jeopardy. Local concerts and entertainment events were postponed. Most central Indiana schools will be open today. **Page A17**

SEARCH AND RESCUE

Massive effort is under way
Families are seeking news. Crews began heading into ground zero to search for survivors and recover bodies. Hundreds of police, firefighters are missing. **Page A8**

COMMERCE

Economists fear a recession
Economists fear the United States — and the world — will be thrown into a recession. But the Fed says its ready to pump extra money into the economy to prevent such a development. **Page A12**

Shaken businesses close
Employees too shaken to work were sent home. Malls and brokerages throughout Indianapolis closed. Companies with workers on the road scrambled to reassure family members. **Page A12**

MASS DESTRUCTION

The terror unfolded quickly
A time line recaps how the events unfolded Tuesday, and photographs capture the nation's horror. **Pages A10, 11**

Go online for updates
Go online for the latest developments in the attacks. In addition, check flight schedules at the airport; see photo galleries and review gas prices at Pump Patrol. **WWW.INDYSTAR.COM**

Copyright 2001
The Star

The Indianapolis Star

Pictures speak a thousand words, and the Indianapolis Star newspaper displays fear, anguish, astonishment, despair and total destruction caused by the hijacked planes that slammed into the towers of the World Trade Center in New York City earlier in the day, September 11, 2001. (AP Photo/The Indianpolis Star)

The Statue of Liberty and the Manhattan skyline of New York City

"The Statue of Liberty shines her torch in New York Harbor as twin towers of light pierce the sky like the ghostly outlines of skyscrapers, capping a solemn day of memorials to the victims of the nation's deadliest act of terrorism, Monday, March 22, 2002. The columns of light were visible for miles. The illuminations marked the six months since the Sept. 11 attacks on the World Trade Center…." The towers of light, known as the "Tribute in Light" memorial, cast their beams each night until April 13, 2002. (AP Photo/U.S. Coast Guard, Petty Officer Tom Sperduto)

A lasting tribute to United Flight 93

"A note rests among flags at a memorial near the crash site of United Flight 93, in Shanksville, Pa., Thursday Oct. 11, 2001. The hijacked airliner crashed Sept. 11, killing all 44 crew and passengers, shortly after two other hijacked airliners crashed into the World Trade Center towers in New York and another into the Pentagon. (AP Photo/Gary Tramontina)